The Real Life of a Church Girl

The Real Life of a Church Girl

THE UNTOLD STORY

By T. J. Callahan

Charleston, SC
www.PalmettoPublishing.com

The Real Life of a Church Girl

Copyright © 2020 by T. J. Callahan

All rights reserved
No portion of this book may be reproduced, stored in a retrieval system, or transmitted in any form by any means–electronic, mechanical, photocopy, recording, or other–except for brief quotations in printed reviews, without prior permission of the author.

Paperback ISBN: 978-1-64990-714-1
eBook ISBN: 978-1-64990-727-1

Dedication

To all the church girls who've had to suffer in silence and couldn't tell their truth in fear of being judged. Today we shall be free of the mask, judgment, and conflict we've had to deal with all our lives. Pray it will bring true change, take away the stigma, and allow us to be the people of God we were created to be. Deliverance, breakthrough, and change will take place. Generational curses shall be destroyed. And your mind, body, and spirits will be strengthened.

I dedicate this book to God. There's never been a moment you haven't been there. I'm truly grateful to you for allowing me to bring this forth. To my three heartbeats, A. J., Ale, and Alaila, for being the reasons why I work to be free to be who God has created me to be, so you can always live your lives free in God. To my sister girls, Jackie, Yar, Jan, Kim Anaissa and my Paradise family, thank you. To my aunt Doris, who's always loved me unconditionally. To my daddy, whose tough love has pushed me to be the best me. To my aunt Jean, who truly worries about me and believes in me and prays for me. To my uncle Mac and uncle Speedy, who love me like I'm truly their daughter. To my siblings—I love you. And to my sister girls, who have always prayed, encouraged, laughed, and loved me—I love you. To my aunt Phyllis, thank you for your prayers, and to my entire family—I love you.

For I know the plans I have for you declares the Lord, "plans to prosper you and not to harm you, plans to give you hope and a future.
—Jeremiah 29:11 (NIV)

Table of Contents

Preface ix
Chapter 1   Bernadette 1
Chapter 2   Change of Life 7
Chapter 3   The Boogie Down 13
Chapter 4   Religion and Reality 19
Chapter 5   The Star 25
Chapter 6   Training 31
Chapter 7   Love and Marriage 35
Chapter 8   Rage Was Her Name 43
Chapter 9   Motherhood through It All 49
Chapter 10 Divorce and Singlehood 55
Chapter 11 2016 61
Chapter 12 Called to Be 67
About the Author 73

Preface

I

Being born into my mother's side of the family, I was expected to live one way: holy. I was surrounded by pastors, elders, ministers, and the saints of God. That was my village; I was a real-life church girl.

From the time I can remember, my life was all-day Sunday church, Wednesday night Bible study, Friday-night service, and Saturday church activities. My way of life, my routine. All I knew and heard were the words *Holy Ghost* and *holiness*. I remember choir members in their black-and-white clothes. "Church women don't wear pants." You had to wear a lace head covering; no fornication or committing adultery was allowed. If you did, you would be silenced and treated differently by the saints of God. All I knew was that the pastor had control of the saints in their church, and if you were a pastor, you had a pretty wife, a nice car and house, and dressed the best. These were my realities with contradictions thrown in the mix.

II

I witnessed feminine men having girlfriends but flirting with men, and while directing the choir, men cheated on their wives. Kids were humping in the bathroom while service was going on. People were doing the holy dance, speaking in tongues, while killing people with their tongues. I knew young that this church thing was not all it was cracked up to be, but the spirit of God was powerful and felt electric and made me cry.

At an early age, I experienced the seed of perversion creeping in suddenly—older men taking advantage of little girls who had no idea of what sex or intimacy was all about. My first time being molested was by a family friend; he was babysitting because my mom had to go to a church revival during the weeknights. This was a person whom my mother trusted with her children. My brother fell asleep, and I was left alone with him. He began to touch me in my private areas. I was no older than seven, so I didn't have breasts; my shape hadn't even formed. So what attracted him to me? It was the first time I saw a man's penis…I thought it was the ugliest thing I had ever lain eyes on.

III

The next day I started to tell my mom what had happened, and before I could finish, she said to me, "Did he touch you in a bad way?" I said, "Yes, Mommy, he did." She questioned him, but nothing came of it. My mom was being a good Christian and didn't press charges. Because of that it put me in a position to be molested once again. This time it was family, and it happened often. He used to finger pop me all the time and say, "Your butt is mine, and there's nothing you can do." I knew it was disgusting, but I felt if I told, it would destroy my mother because he and she were so close. I kept that a secret until I was nineteen years old, when what I once buried started resurfacing. I would be in random places, and the memory or feeling would come over me, and I would just clench my vagina. It started affecting me to the point I felt nasty, dirty, and ashamed.

One day this bad feeling was so overwhelming that all I could do was cry out to the Lord and say, "Deliver me from this awful feeling. Deliver me, God, from a bad spirit that had begun to make me feel so small."

IV

God began to heal and set me free. Once I released it, I exposed it and told a family member. She believed me and confronted him. He sort of apologized, but it didn't matter because I finally acknowledged that what he did, I didn't deserve, and it wasn't my fault. His brokenness didn't diminish my worth.

There are so many broken people possessing and infecting other people with their brokenness all while shouting loud, "I'm Christian; I'm saved, a baptized believer." This type of demonic behavior must be addressed, exposed, and cast out so that people can live and not just exist.

Chapter 1

BERNADETTE

My mom was an usher—the head usher, to be exact. A gray-eyed high, yellow, beautiful single mother of two, my brother Kweku and me, from Harlem, New York. She herself was a church girl born into a world of religious beliefs but very few breakthroughs.

Bernadette Rochelle McCovery was born to Fred McCovery and Pearle McCovery; they were from Alabama. Mommy never really knew her dad; she was the youngest of six, and he denied her from birth. My mother grew up being catered to by her mother and siblings but longed for the love of her father. I remember when my mom lost her sister, my aunt Betty. That was the first time she talked to her father in almost thirty-four years. Even in her sick state, she was losing her battle with cancer herself, but she still was like a little girl hearing her father's voice over the phone. What made it sad was that he wasn't really interested in seeing her, and I could see the hurt in her face. She died about seventy-five days later, never receiving her dad's love.

I witnessed my mother going through life going to church every week, being the nicest person she could be to everyone she came in contact with, but she was never truly set free from the hurt she had endured throughout her life. I remember one Friday after church my mom took home a gentlemen from the church who in my nine year old opinion had an odor and never was groomed well. I was so mad at her an embarrassed because my church friends were laughing. My mother took him home allowed him to bathed, gave him clean clothes and fed him. He stayed the entire weekend and he was so grateful. My mom had the biggest heart and never hurt anyone intentionally, even though she was hurting. Back then I feel like most church people didn't talk about their deep issues. They just thought because they were now saved and filled with the Holy Ghost, all of their issues were gone, but they were sadly mistaken. Mom was going through rejection, cancer, loneliness, a broken marriage, a miscarriage, a stillborn baby, abuse—just to name a few. She never complained, and maybe she didn't know how to talk about it; instead, she would be comical, and she suffered in silence. And through her example I learned how to go through hurt and pain and suffer in silence myself.

Mommy was sick, and I had different caregivers and people who used my mother's sickness to take advantage of my innocence. I was molested twice by a man. One was a family member and the other was a family friend, opening my sexual awareness before it was time to. I never wanted to hurt my mother by telling her, especially about one of them whom she trusted the most. I suffered in silence and didn't say anything to anyone until I was almost nineteen years old. I was being a good church girl instead of telling my father or one of my uncles, who would have knocked them out. I kept quiet, not realizing those marks would come back and haunt me in the future.

During my mother's sickness, she was in and out of the hospital and taking chemotherapy, which pulled out all of her hair. Three years leading up to that day, I experienced my mother having numerous home attendants, bedsores, and pain. She was in her early thirties, losing all her beauty slowly. I remember my sixth-grade graduation.

My mom was in a wheelchair because her feet had swelled up so big. She was only thirty-four, but she looked like an old woman. I imagine the pain and fear she must have been in. She knew she would have to leave her children to be taken care of by other people.

The Real Life of a Church Girl

I entered the seventh grade in September of 1987, and I was so excited that I was finally allowed to travel on my own by bus. I remember it was a long weekend. I asked my mother if I could visit my dad's house for a little while that Monday. She was apprehensive but eventually gave in and let me go. I was so busy trying to get to my father's house that I really didn't take out time to make sure she was OK and love on her. That evening before, when I was leaving to go back home from my father's, my dad came in the room to let me know my mother was taken to the hospital and that I was going to stay at his house for a few days. By that Saturday I was still there. My dad's wife had a sweet sixteen to attend, and we all went. It was a rainy night. We returned from the party, and we got in the house late, so I went straight to sleep.

At about 4:00 a.m., I had a dream that my mother had died. I saw her in a white casket with a pretty white dress on. That morning my dad walked into the room, and the look of sadness and pain on his face made me say, "I know, Daddy; my mother died." He confirmed this.

October 4, 1987, was by far the worst day of my life. After years of battling with cancer, my mom passed away at thirty-four years old. That began my life of anxiety, fear, distrust, and sadness because my mommy didn't get better. Things were just changing, and there was nothing I could do about it. As I grew up in the church, the saints and my aunts would come over the house and pray for her healing, but God didn't let her get healed; she just kept dying. I feel like I was losing my trust in God because the one person who had my back was leaving me slowly. When I was eleven years old, I was taught directly to suffer in silence, but I developed a strong fear and belief that even if things were going well, something bad would end up happening, so I stopped expecting good things to happen. I really began to live a life of a church girl—always smiling, being nice, never really complaining, praying but not expecting change, basically settling and never questioning anything. **Have you ever experienced trauma? IF so, how did you deal with the trauma?**

Real Talk and Reflection

Real Talk and Reflection

Real Talk and Reflection

Chapter 2

CHANGE OF LIFE

Shortly after my mom died, I entered a different way of life. This was a different situation from living with my mom and brother. I was eleven years old. I had just lost my mother; had moved into a really religious home; and was separated from my brother, school, church, and my best friends, Jennifer, Shinelle, and Joyce, and everything I once knew. I felt abandoned and sad. I came from living with my single mom taking care of everything to moving into a two-parent, two-income household with five male cousins. I went from being the center of attention to just being the extra mouth to feed. I had been attending the same church for nine years of my life to now attending a completely different church: new people, new kids to get along with, and different traditions to get used to. My identity was stripped from me, and I had no say-so. Decisions made by the adults in my life were, I guess, the best that they knew how to do. Today I wish that my dad, his wife, and all of my uncles and aunts would have sat down and really thought about how their decisions would affect me in the long run.

I was eleven and wasn't provided the tools to grieve. I believe I entered into the world of wearing a mask. I was in someone else's life, not living but just surviving, and I would not exit that world until I was in my forties.

I was separated from my brother and my protector, which was also very traumatic for me. My brother was made an adult at the age of fifteen. He, too, had lost his mother, and his father wasn't very present. I so admire my brother because he always strives to be better and to take care of his family. He is a fighter and a hustler; he is smart and extremely personable. He has become a great man; our mother would be so proud.

The first year in Queens was rough, and I was sad most of the time. I felt trapped, and I wanted out. I endured a lot of emotional challenges and changes, but my favorite boy cousin, Ahmad, made life seem not so bad. We were two peas in a pod. I don't think he really understood how much I depended on him. He had my back, and I his. I was able to be myself with him and tell him my secrets. We shared food (beef patties and coco bread), always conjuring up plans and adventures. He may never understand the place he holds in my heart.

My uncle was a provider and protector. He truly loved his family and never hurt or took advantage of me, but he always appeared angry and serious. I can remember he was a creature of habit, always going food shopping weekly, making up his ground-beef patties, and bringing home pizza and garlic knots every Thursday. I loved to watch him eat. He made every meal seem so delicious. My uncle wasn't yet living for Christ when I first moved in with the family, so he was always unhappy and seemed to be in a battle. Having a father figure in the home was already different. Some days I lay in bed wishing I could wake up out of this terrible dream. No one was hurting me or anything, but I was so sad and shattered over the death of my mother. I didn't know how to express the feelings, and no one ever came to assist me with sorting out her death.

My aunt was one of the sweetest people I knew. And she loved God and had such a unique spiritual connection to God. My aunt had five boys of her own, so when I came to live with them, that gave her six children to care for—plus, I was a girl. This had to be challenging and overwhelming for her. She wasn't a stay-at-home mom; she was a New York City public school teacher. As Christians we usually just grin and bear things, no matter what we feel like, even if we don't agree. I guess we feel like somehow it makes us a bad Christian to say no. I know my aunt loved me, but I am not sure if she truly was in total agreement to take me on full time.

I was used to my mom's affection and nurturing; that was gone. My aunt and uncle were not overly affectionate hugging-kissing types of people, but they showed me their love by making sure I had what I needed, and for that I'm so grateful to them. Living with five boys and never being around girls other than school was weird for me, and I felt like I was missing out on something. The decision was made for me to live with my father and his family in the Bronx. **How do you deal with change?**

Real Talk and Reflection

Real Talk and Reflection

Real Talk and Reflection

Chapter 3

THE BOOGIE DOWN

Moving to the Bronx meant no more church activities. I was watching soaps in the evening my dad had taped during the day to watch with his wife. There were Budweiser, "reefah" and bamboo paper, and wine coolers involved. This was different for the first time in my life. No gospel music was being played in my house; it was replaced with jazz and R&B. Again, I was in the situation of being with a female figure who wasn't affectionate, and now I was twelve and really missing my mother's love. I was looking for relief. My heart was truly broken, and no one was caring for that part of me.

I didn't know at the time, but my dad was dealing with drug addiction. He was what you would call a functioning addict. He worked for sanitation but was an addict. My dad was a tough-love dad, plus his emotions were up and down due to his addiction.

My dad exposed me to black culture and the love of being black. I went to the Harlem School of the Arts. I learned ethnic, jazz, and modern dance. I also learned in chorus and drama classes. I was exposed to children of doctors and lawyers, politicians, and future models and TV stars. That performance arts school allowed me to see black beauty. I will forever be grateful to my father for that gift.

T. J. Callahan

My stepmom, a cute little curvy, petite lady, was hard in my opinion, and I didn't feel at the time that she really liked me or wanted me to live with them. In retrospect, now looking back and seeing things with adult eyes, my stepmother was dealing with a heroin-addicted husband who now had put another responsibility on her. She was going through her own personal hell and now was dealing with another teenage girl who was completely different from her daughters. It probably was a challenge she didn't really feel like dealing with. I feel she handled it the best way she could at that time. I learned structure from her and how to keep house. And something I do to this day is take baths to clean my inside parts.

I loved living in the Bronx. I no longer felt like I was a hostage. Being able to go outside and explore the streets with my friend Lola was amazing. Most of the street smarts I know, I learned in this time period of time. I went to the best house parties. During that time I didn't want to be a part of the church world; I completely disassociated myself with Christianity but continued to live wearing a mask. I was learning to adapt in any situation I was put in. I was walking around this world broken and numb. Thank God I was blessed with Lola who had a part in making my life easier. She was and is to this day genuine, and we have become sisters for life.

The year I was to enter high school, my dad had to go away into rehab for six to nine months; from what I can remember, that left me feeling abandoned all over again. Entering into tenth grade at Norman Thomas High School, I wasn't ready. The kids were dressed like grown people with all the latest styles and fashions; I felt like a fish out of water. I wasn't mentally prepared for this kind of atmosphere. My dad was away, my stepmother and I weren't getting along, and I didn't have the clothes to make me feel confident to be a part of the school. I eventually cut school half of the year. I stayed at my friend's house and watched movies. I didn't realize at the time I was depressed, and I used those movies to escape from everything I was dealing with. By the end of my tenth-grade year, my stepmother and I had a bad argument, and my uncle Mac was called. The decision was made for me to return and live back with my family in Queens. This would be the beginning of years of religion, bad decisions, estranged family relationships, and me experiencing the realities of life. My dad wasn't happy I moved back to live with my uncle and aunt. One of my biggest regrets is holding a grudge against my father as long as I did. **Do you hold grudges? How do you deal with uncomfortable situations?**

Real Talk and Reflection

Real Talk and Reflection

Real Talk and Reflection

Chapter 4

RELIGION AND REALITY

Now the second time around, living with my uncle and aunt was completely different. They now had a new baby girl, who had been born with a rare heart condition. My uncle was saved and sanctified, and the church services were being held in our house. I felt religiously smothered. My aunt was definitely a sweet and powerful woman of God, living her spiritual life the best way she knew, but I felt like I couldn't be myself. There was no more listening to worldly music, dancing, wearing pants or jewelry, or braiding my hair, because in 1 Timothy 2:9 (KJV) says, "In like manner also, that women adorn themselves in modest apparel, with shamefacedness and sobriety; not with braided hair, or gold, or pearls, or costly array." The biggest thing was that I was no longer allowed to attend movie theaters. Psalm 1:1 (NIV) says, "Blessed is the man who does not walk in the counsel of the wicked or stand in the way of sinners or sit in the seat of mockers. But his delight is in the law of the LORD, and on his law he meditates day and night."

It felt like I was stripped immediately. I remember coming home from school and going into my drawers to change my clothes, and all my pants were gone. I was told no more pants were allowed to be worn in the household. My aunt not only said it to me, but she said it in front of her church girlfriends. I felt humiliated, embarrassed, hurt, and alone. My big cousin Akin spoke up for me because he saw my face, but it was to no avail, so I just shut up and suffered in silence. That day I began to convince myself that this way of thinking was the right way and the way I would see Jesus one day.

My cousin's and my relationship changed a bit. Now looking back, I think he probably put up walls because I left him to move to the Bronx with my dad. I never realized he may have felt abandoned by me because I had left, and he'd needed me just like I needed him.

Now everything felt like a competition: Who was more saved? Who was filled with the Holy Ghost? Who had read their Bible more? Who prayed in the prayer room longer? This wasn't real relationship building; this was mimicking, not really understanding true relationship with God. In the midst of all of this praying, speaking in tongues, and reading the Bible, there was discord going on in the household, and this was conflicting to me. I didn't understand how in one breath we could be talking about God's anointing and love, and in the next breath, we were allowed not to talk and deal with issues. I was learning how to be a church girl.

Now in my eleventh-grade year, I was the church girl—Bible toting, long skirt wearing, no longer cutting classes. My entire attitude changed. This was positive because the previous year, I had been making horrible decisions that were taking me down the wrong path. My school friends surprisingly loved the church girl. They definitely respected my change and were curious to learn about this God I was serving. I began to teach Bible study and talk about the goodness of God. I didn't realize then that God had given me a love for souls who were broken and damaged and needed someone to talk with them and not judge what they were doing. At school I felt free to be who God was calling me to be, but at home I felt like I was religiously bound up. No doubt the teaching and spirit were real, but my understanding of real life and real-life issues and how to deal with them were blurred. By the time I graduated high school, my heart was yearning to change my environment. It was not that I didn't love my family, because I definitely loved them, but I knew inside that my territory needed to be enlarged. The decision was made for me to move with other family members, which led me to join the Star. **Have you ever felt like you were in a spiritual competition?**

Real Talk and Reflection

Real Talk and Reflection

Real Talk and Reflection

Chapter 5

THE STAR

My first introduction to Morning Start Full Gospel Assembly was years ago when I was a child in Harlem and it was called Morning Star Baptist Church. There were only a handful of members, and most I had known since birth.

Reconnecting to the Star at eighteen years old was definitely a new experience. They moved to the Bronx and had a big congregation, and there was a lot more religious freedom than I was used to. I wasn't prepared for it, but it was exciting and eye-opening. Spiritually, the teaching was the same, but my understanding of the word was opened up better. In comparison, the Star was more liberal than my Queens church. The women wore pants, jewelry, and braids in their hair and listened to worldly along with gospel music. People were having fun and being saved; this was a whole new adventure.

I'm not going to lie. I came into the Star judging everyone; in my opinion they weren't really saved and sanctified like I was taught to be. Some of them were having sex and had babies out of wedlock. I looked at them differently like I was better because I was a virgin. I was a good church girl. I couldn't have been more wrong. Who was I to judge I had my own dirt in my closet that I wasn't dealing with? Coming to the Star made me face some of my hidden sin tendencies. I didn't know how to relate to these young ladies. I had been in such a religious bubble for so long that I was scared to sneeze for fear of sinning. But I was sinning: I was judging, and because I wasn't having sex, I felt like I was a good Christian.

The reality is I hadn't lived a normal life. I lived such a sheltered life that my choices were made for me indirectly. I wasn't put in tempting situations until I came into the Star. It was a learning experience; it made me see things I wouldn't normally look for. I felt like I had been living in Amish country, and now I was a part of Western civilization. I wasn't prepared for the real world. I looked and acted like I was taught to act. I was afraid to get in trouble and go to hell, but in my heart I secretly was curious about a lot of things that were "worldly."

When I met my children's father, my standards were all on me and not really what I expected of him. I was a virgin; I was nice, sweet—a square, pretty much, and proud of it. I didn't really have a standard set for him; I had no expectations. He was saved, and he liked me. Period. He immediately wanted me. I now question whether it was because I was so pure, or whether it was because he knew that he could get over on me because I had no life experiences. Maybe it was both. Either way, life was about to make itself known to me. Quickly I got involved with him, and my views began to change because now I wanted to have sex, go to the movies, and wear pants, jewelry, and braids in my hair. All the traditional ways I was taught were being challenged, and this freedom felt good.

Being a part of a church is way more than the lifting of hands, praising God, reading the word, worshipping, listening to the choir, and so on. A big part of the church experience is the church family. It can be a good and bad thing. The good is that you meet and bond with great people. The bad is that you can sometimes not deal with your biological family. That's what happened to me. I bonded and treated my church family like they were my blood and was distant from my biological family for years. I had family members who were a part of my church family, but even them I could have been closer to. I realize there were certain issues I wasn't dealing with, subconsciously replacing my family because I didn't want to deal with my past.

The Real Life of a Church Girl

In my past there was hurt, abandonment, shame, and bitterness, among other things. I soon would see that attaching myself to new people would bring forth new issues. You began to attach yourself to people, places, and things that God didn't ordain, and you find yourself in a worse state and more broken than you were.

I appreciate my sisters in Christ who loved me and became my homie Kim. Jan took in my children and me and never charged, and they genuinely prayed for my well-being. But I had some heartbreak as well. People I genuinely love and cared for didn't appreciate it, even though it cost them nothing.

The dating and courting process was amazing for the most part. He took care of me, from buying my underwear to my coats and shoes. He took me on my first date to Venus Italian Restaurant in the Bronx. He always made me feel special. He was great with children; he even ran a community basketball gym two times a week and was extremely active in the church. Sure, there were hints and signs that my ex-husband had some issues. He could turn on and off his emotions when he felt like it. I can remember during our engagement one day, out of the blue he came to me and said, "I don't have any feelings for you." He said he didn't know when they would come back. I was devastated and felt so abandoned by him—a young church girl who didn't understand her worth at the time. No matter who told me I was beautiful and told me all that I had going for me, I still longed for his validation. This man who was broken as well was able to dictate my state of mind just like a puppeteer. He was cold, and he treated me like all the love we shared didn't matter. I was so young and inexperienced that I went along with it and experienced a deep depression. I developed irritable bowel syndrome and lost twenty pounds because I couldn't keep anything down. And then out of nowhere, his feelings miraculously came back, and he wanted me again. I was so grateful and immediately took him back instead of dropping him like a bad habit. These on-again-off-again feelings for me would go on for years, and because I had issues myself, I dealt with it. I didn't have anyone protecting me and warning him that if he hurt me, he would be dealt with. I hid it like a good church girl and married him.

T. J. Callahan

The Star helped me step up my game. The young people were educated, searching for their spiritual purpose and not afraid to speak their peace. I learned how to talk in front of a crowd, recognize the things of the spirit, teach, worship and exhort people to praise God. After service praise parties were everything true breakthroughs took place. Men and women preaching and teaching the word of God week after week was amazing and inspiring.

At the Star I learned how to conduct business, went on some the best trips of my life with my church friends. I was living my best and worst life at the same time. **What is your church experience? Did it make you or break you?**

Real Talk and Reflection

Real Talk and Reflection

Chapter 6

TRAINING

The Star also reconnected me with my aunt Doris, my mother's only living sister. She is definitely the perfect model of a church girl who knows who she is. She showed me how to be a true lady, wife, and mother. She showed me so much love that I hadn't experienced since my mother died. I was able to share pretty much all of my dark secrets with her, and she never judged me as a woman. She held me to high standards and corrected me when she felt I was wrong and would fight for me when she felt someone was coming against me. She is my ride-or-die chick definitely. She carried me in the spirit and showed how to be authentic in God. To be honest, until God allowed me to be around my aunt, I didn't really understand my place in God. I didn't understand the way spirit could move and how the power of God could truly change your life. Because I was her armor bearer, I was exposed to a higher level of the spirit. But because I still had some generational curses attached to me that I wouldn't allow myself to deal with, I continued to struggle to be consistent and walk in my calling.

I was in training to become a powerful woman of God, but I couldn't receive it fully. I now realize I was fearful. I feared failing and succeeding. I had been in a place of lost and defeat for so long, I didn't know how to recognize the blessing of God. God continued to send me prophetic words, but I was stuck and subconsciously refused to take God at his word. I would go through a tough journey. **Why don't we allow ourselves to live?**

Real Talk and Reflection

Real Talk and Reflection

Chapter 7

LOVE AND MARRIAGE

I wasn't prepared for this chapter of my life. On October 11, 1997, I was married to my children's father. My wedding dress was beautiful, and I thought it was the beginning of a beautiful high with the man I loved so much. If anybody would have told me what I was about to endure for the next ten years or so, I probably wouldn't have believed them. I had no idea what dark hole I was entering and by the time I realized it, I had no idea how to get out.

Growing up in church, all you heard was it's better to marry than to burn or not be unequally yoked. I had to be submissive to my husband, be faithful to the church, know my role, and stay in my lane. None of this prepared me for the dose of reality that comes with a real-life broken marriage.

Being compatible, dealing with issues and generational curses, being trustworthy, and having positive structure, honesty, and unconditional love should have been some of the prerequisites accomplished before saying, "I do." We said the words during the ceremony; then once we left the altar, those words were picked and chosen when it was convenient. Real life soon crept in, and real issues showed up and showed out.

I didn't have the true understanding of who I was, and now I was in the role of helpmate. I thought being a helpmate was tolerating and agreeing with whatever my husband did and accepting it because he was the head. It was my duty to hide all of the crap he dealt to me because I had been taught that what happens at home stays at home. I couldn't have been more wrong. "Helpmate" doesn't mean "doormat." It doesn't mean helping with continuing the cycle of bad behaviors. My not saying anything kept the bad cycle going, and that was a recipe for disaster.

Being the head of a household wasn't as simple as marking "head of household" while doing taxes. A man being placed at the head of household comes with serious responsibilities. It means being the ruler, disciplinarian, breadwinner, and protector, making wise and final decisions. I don't feel he was equipped to fulfill his role. I don't place the blame on him; these were deep-rooted seeds that were planted and never addressed, childhood traumas that were never talked about. I don't think even he understood the magnitude of the hurt, pain, and brokenness that was attached to his life. We both had generational curses we came into the marriage with, curses that didn't surface until we said, "I do." Yes, two "saved" people. Yes, me, "the church girl" with a generational curse attached to my life and the lives of our future children. We had no business getting married.

I had my own childhood traumas: being molested, Mom's death, and Dad being on drugs, all happening before I turned thirteen. These were generational curses that came down from my great-grandmother, grandmother, and mother having broken marriages—women not knowing their self-worth and accepting disrespect and disappointment after disappointment as if it were normal.

He and I never really talked about any of our previous traumas, which left us open for divorce, infidelity, sadness, disappointment, hurt, devastation, witchcraft, embarrassment, perversion, mental health issues, and emotional, verbal, and financial abuse. I never really experienced peace in my marriage, but I remained silent and always had humor on my tongue. I was a good church girl, smiling and rarely complaining, and I often made excuses and felt that it was my duty as a good Christian woman to take it.

My wedding night was scary because I was a virgin. To be honest sex wasn't great because it was just that: sex. There was no lovemaking—just sex...me following instructions from my leader. I hated sex. I felt like I never knew what I was doing. Then the issue of porn was introduced. That made it even worse because I now had to compete with a porn star who had sex for a living. Again I don't place blame; some men are taught that porn is normal and is a way to make their sex lives spicy. But the truth is that porn and the spirits that come along with porn can destroy and put separation in a relationship. And that's exactly what it did in my marriage from the beginning. I never felt comfortable with watching it, and I was made to feel like I was a cornball or acting like a little girl who didn't want to please her man. Eventually this issue was brought to my pastor, who happened to be my uncle and whom my husband worshipped. I was a young wife who felt like she was bullied into watching porn and performing the acts. So, yes, I told my pastor during a counseling session, and my ex-husband hated me for saying anything and embarrassing him. He vowed that day that he would never trust me and treat me the same, and literally he kept his vow throughout the entire marriage.

I became pregnant six months after we got married. I was still in school, and my husband was the only one bringing income into our home. He did what he needed to take care of me and our child, but it became overwhelming for him being an active husband, father, bread winner and fulfilling all his church duties. He wanted to be obedient to authority and gave up job opportunities, and this led to a lot of financial hardships and brought issues into our marriage.

When my first child was born, it was the happiest time of my life I finally had someone who loved me unconditionally, who depended on me, and whom I could trust. But with this new baby came new responsibility and pressure for my husband. We moved into a beautiful three bedroom apartment with French doors, and a big dining room and living room. It seemed like things were good, but they weren't. Then generational curses began to show their ugly faces. That apartment was the beginning of the darkest times in my life. How could I be going to church every Wednesday, Friday, and all day Sunday, and have all this darkness happen in my life? Yes, I was the bishop's and pastor's niece, but it didn't matter. Those generational curses were not addressed, so I didn't even know what I was up against so I could fight it. I now realize that when attaching yourself to a person, you better know what they are working with spiritually, if you are not prepared, it could destroy you.

My husband had ambition and wanted to start a Christian production company, incorporating gospel shows—gospel on wheels—and creating a choir. It was something that could've been amazing, but I don't think the church at the time was ready for these new-age changes. Looking back now, I think that one of the things that broke him down, and he started craving worldly things.

Once my second child was born, my ex-husband and I separated. I cut off all my hair, started wearing pants, and tried to regain my sanity. But deep down I wanted my husband and my family to be together. During our separation, a curveball was thrown: my ex-husband had a child outside the marriage not even a year after I had my second child.

Yes, I took him back because I wanted to save my family. I thought finally he would give me the respect and love I longed for from him, because I did a big thing by taking him back and taking his child as my own. It did the opposite. It showed him how to treat me. Subconsciously, I told him he could do whatever he wanted to me. No matter what, I would take him back. I thought I was being a good Christian wife. Even though I was losing my mind, I smiled and did my church thing, and even in the midst of all of that, I had my daughter.

When my baby girl turned three months old, my marriage was in its worst state. On January 22, while taking the children to school in Harlem, I was in such a broken, sad, and tired state of mind. It was a cold morning, and I heard a voice say, "Put the plush teddy bear snowsuit on the baby." I was obedient and put her in the snowsuit. We took the D train to 145th street and St. Nicholas Avenue. As I was walking up the steps to go out the exit, others passengers were running down the steps trying to catch the train. One passenger pushed past me, which caused me to lose my balance. I turned around, trying to gain my balance, and I knew at that point I was going to fall, but I had my baby strapped on me. To avoid crushing her, I had to fall in a way that was going to hurt me but save her. We were rushed to Presbyterian Hospital; my children were in one ambulance, and I was in another. It was one of the most traumatic events my children and I had to experience. Thank God, my baby was fine. My son A. J. protected my baby like he was a grown man. I, on the other hand, had a shattered tibia. I had to get reconstructive surgery and now have two plates and four screws in my right leg for life. The incident not only left me with physical scars but emotional ones as well. To this day it's difficult to recall that day.

While I was in the hospital, God began to show me that he wasn't an in-the-box kind of God. I remember watching TBN, a Christian station, and seeing people of God praising God in different ways. I saw Christians with tattoos worshipping God. These people didn't look traditional, but you could feel the anointing through the television. I knew that God had called me to be an out-of-the-box Christian. But because I was still in this unstable state of mind, I continued not to walk in my place in God.

Returning home from the hospital, I had wonderful people who took care my children. I can't really tell you what state of mind my ex-husband was in. At first he was helping with my recovery, but then that help ended, and a shift took place. I remember it was his birthday, and the children were staying with friends because I couldn't walk and care for them. It got late, and I needed my pain medicine. From my bedroom I could see the medication on the table, but I couldn't walk to it. I suffered all night in pain, and my body almost went into shock. During the course of the night, I called my ex on the phone begging him to come home to give me the medication, but he refused. Thank God I survived and made it through that chapter of my life.

Drugs didn't make me leave, his attitude didn't make me leave, cheating didn't make me leave, and verbal abuse didn't make me leave. In fact I was convinced my marriage was going to be made whole, because whenever I lost hope my ex would become Mr. wonderful again. One year I would be a part of the married couples' group, and then the next year the singles. In my mind if I let it go, that would mean I didn't believe God could fix it. I felt like a failure. I had to face it. This man didn't love or respect me; he was broken and hurt. Hurt people, hurt people.

Finally it was our ten-year anniversary, we were blessed with Broadway tickets to see *The Color Purple*. We got a babysitter, and even though our marriage was not in great shape, I continued to have hope. After the play was over, I thought he would take me out to a romantic dinner. Instead he stopped at Wendy's, drove to our building, dropped me off, and went out for the rest of the night. I went upstairs, and for the first time, I didn't cry or have a pity party. I made a decision to end the marriage. I knew at that moment that all of my hopes and dreams of keeping my family together were ridiculous. There was no love, respect, happiness, or trust in this marriage, and I had to change the atmosphere for my children. I didn't want my sons to think it was OK to treat women badly, and I didn't want my daughter to feel like she had to be treated badly in order to keep a man. I knew that I had to break the cycle.

Even though I ended the relationship I continued to hold on. It took me six months to file for divorce. Up until that time, he still had the key to the apartment. We continued to have sex every once in a while. I was fearful to truly end the relationship because I was holding on to the man I met when I was eighteen years old who treated me nice. Issues were not accurately addressed and dealt with so healing couldn't take place. Once I really began to trust God, it became easier to end that chapter. And once I really ended it, I've never considered looking back. True deliverance had taken place.

I exposed my pass because healing needs to take place and broken relationships need to be restored. Please don't leave this chapter with a negative view of marriage. Marriage can be a wonderful experience when it's healthy. It's important to address the issues even when they are uncomfortable, because the issues won't go anywhere. Don't get married just to have a beautiful wedding, just to have sex or so you won't be single. Love yourself, get to know who you are and most of all be prayerful. **Why do we stay in unhealthy situations? What is your idea of a healthy marriage?**

Real Talk and Reflection

Real Talk and Reflection

Chapter 8

RAGE WAS HER NAME

After going through my marriage, I developed this ugly thing called rage. Because I allowed my ex-husband to treat me any kind of way, I would lash out at anyone who made me feel threatened. All of that suppressed energy, I didn't take out on him; I took out on any man who I felt disrespected me. I hated myself because I was turning into a monster. I was angry and would go from zero to a hundred in seconds. I was broken inside but still smiling like everything was OK. I began to put myself and my children in positions in which we could've been hurt or even killed, because I would challenge any man; it didn't matter who or where I was. I remember flinging a bottle at a store owner's head because he didn't answer me right and challenging a cab driver because he was trying to overcharge me, which led him to speed off with me in the car, taking me away from my destination. He could have taken me somewhere and raped and killed me, and the whole time, I was going off making the situation worse. During this whole time, I was leading devotional and being faithful to the ministry, while anger, bitterness, and rage were growing by the second.

Before I knew it, I was acting a fool in church, and I would tell somebody in a minute to shut up before I punched them in the face, especially if I felt disrespected. In my mind I wasn't going to allow another person to make me feel belittled ever again. I was willing to risk my life as long as I was able to get that person back. I was suffering from a mental health issue, and I didn't even recognize at the time that's what it was.

Mental health includes our emotional, psychological, and social well-being. It affects how we think, feel, and act. It also helps determine how we handle stress, relate to others, and make choices. Mental health is important at every stage of life, from childhood and adolescence through adulthood.

Over the course of your life, if you experience mental health problems, you're thinking, mood, and behavior could be affected. Many factors contribute to mental health problems—biological factors, such as genes or brain chemistry; life experiences, such as trauma or abuse; or a family history of mental health problems.

I wasn't dealing with it and was playing the blame game and not owning up to my contribution. Yes, things had been done to me that were not right. Yes, I was mentally, emotionally, and financially abused. Yes, I was made to feel like I was nothing. I taught my ex how to treat me. The first time he disrespected me, I should nipped it immediately. I was taught as a Christian woman, you have to be submissive to your husband. "Submissive" doesn't mean be a doormat. In the word it speaks on this subject in Colossians 3:18 and 19 (NIV) "Wives, submit yourselves to your husbands, as is fitting in the Lord." In the next verse, it states, "Husbands, love your wives and do not be harsh with them." Had I first been obedient to the word of God, it would have shielded me from years of abuse, rage, bitterness, and low self-esteem. Just because you are born in the church and are a church girl or boy, it doesn't guarantee your relationship with God. Truly spending that time, fasting, praying, and reading God's word is what guarantees the relationship and deliverance over your life. In Matthew 17:21(KJV) it states, "Howbeit this kind goth not out but by prayer and fasting." That's what I was lacking: the relationship with God. I was mostly *doing* and lacking the *being* part.

One day I decided to look Tamica Jataun Callahan in the face and take accountability for my life and all of the things I needed to do to mend my broken pieces. I had to let go of pride, anger, fear, jealousy, rage, low self-esteem, blame, pity, and hatred, among other things.

I had to let go of the anger and jealousy I had because my ex-husband had gotten remarried. I didn't want him back—but how dare he be married, having matrimonial sex, and I was sitting there struggling not to fornicate? I had to let go of the fact that my ex-husband's mistress was married to a good dude and was living what appeared to be a good life. For a time that messed my head up. I felt so low, like I didn't deserve happiness. The more I got closer to God, the more he showed me that their marriages had nothing to do with me. We all have our own journeys, and it wasn't my business to worry about theirs. I had to let it go. **Have you ever dealt with Anger issues or Rage? Are you afraid of the stigma of mental health?**

Real Talk and Reflection

Real Talk and Reflection

Real Talk and Reflection

Chapter 9

MOTHERHOOD THROUGH IT ALL

I became a mother at twenty-four years old. It was one of the best things that ever happened to me. A. J. was an eight-pound-one-ounce beautiful baby boy. Finally I had someone who depended on me and loved me no matter what. Motherhood was great, but the journey of being a wife, mother, and woman of God wasn't all I hoped it to be.

When I got married, I was a size twelve after having my son and even breastfeeding I did not snap back like most women I knew. I got on birth control and went up to a size twenty-four. I had never experienced feeling bad about my body image; I didn't recognize myself in pictures or even my own reflection in the mirror. I went from a 34C breast size to 42DD breast size, feeling ugly and unattractive. There would be times in church that I felt so low, but I wore a mask, never experiencing my brokenness. When that music came on, I would break out in a shout, trying to get those bad feelings off me. I didn't quite know how to deal with all that was coming my way. What I did know how to do was smile and laugh, even in the pain.

In the midst of scary and uncomfortable feelings, I knew how to be a mommy. It came so naturally to me as long, as my baby was good. I learned how to cope. I would go on to breastfeed A. J. for seventeen months because I didn't want to let go of that bond; it was my comfort zone.

T. J. Callahan

Finally, when I finished breastfeeding, I resumed my duties in ministry. I was a devotional leader, youth leader, pastor's aide, Sunday school teacher, and women's leader. My ex-husband was a pastor's aide, Sunday school teacher, trustee, head of the cleanup crew, and usher. We were the first ones at church and the last ones to leave. On a typical Sunday, we were so busy between services, taking care of the bishop and pastor and in and out of meetings, we didn't have time to feed our baby. Thank God for Auntie Jan. We were doing instead of being, and it showed up especially when we were behind closed doors.

We moved a couple of houses down from where we were living—a beautiful apartment with three bedrooms, a dining room, a living room, French doors, and one bathroom and kitchen. I remember my baby and myself being in that apartment. I was sad, and a heavy spirit rested in that apartment. We were in the church, doing and looking like everything was great and we were at the top of our game, but it wasn't great. We were losing the game, with a one-year-old witnessing the madness. I had to eventually move in with my mother-in-law because rent was not being paid. I finally had A. J. away from the dark spirit that was in that apartment. As a young mother, I didn't really know what was going on at the time. I realize the devil was trying to destroy my life and the life of my child. Mothers, pray over your children; sometimes you won't see the effect until years later.

Two years and eleven months later, Ale Nathaniel Wilson was born. A week before he was born, my children's father decided to give up the church life, which left me in devastation. During that time, my husband would come and care for the children. They loved their dad and always wanted to be around him. I always welcomed it because I wanted my family.

On October 4, 2006, my beautiful daughter, Alaila Bernadette, came into this world looking just like my mother. What are the odds she would be born the same date my mother passed away? Motherhood hasn't been easy but has been so worth it.

Being a mother when you are experiencing brokenness is difficult because even when you are an excellent mother, your children still feel your brokenness, and it sometimes becomes their brokenness. We teach our children how to love, hate, cope, and deal with life, expectations, anxiety, and victories. I've learned in my motherhood journey to be honest, to stop fronting, and to prepare my children because they already know what the deal is. But when we withhold and shelter them, we do not prepare them for life and the possible obstacles they could endure. I've learned to support but not to overcompensate, to correct but not control, to mostly encourage them to put God first and develop their own relationship with God because that's going to be the key factor on this journey called life. **What are we teaching our children? Has your secrets affected your children?**

Real Talk and Reflection

Real Talk and Reflection

Real Talk and Reflection

Chapter 10

DIVORCE AND SINGLEHOOD

When I was thirty-four, I filed for divorce. It was one of the best decisions I've made. The only thing I regret is my children had to endure a detached father and a mom who overcompensates because of lack. And I didn't prepare them when they were younger about the realities of life because I was a hindrance, and I covered things up and made the package look so good.

Divorce made me feel like a failure and no longer a part of the "in crowd" in church. Being so young and divorced was embarrassing. I even had a mother in the church say to me, "Your husband left you because you gained so much weight." She was so wrong, but her words hurt because I felt that's probably what other people were thinking. As people of purpose, we have to build one another up. In 1 Thessalonians 5:11 (NIV), it states, "Therefore encourage one another and build each other up, just as in fact you are doing." Just because I had papers didn't mean I had freedom. Even after the divorce, I tried to keep everything together like holidays, and when we were in public, I acted like we were best friends, but I wasn't addressing the issues, so they were still following us. I felt that as long as my children were comfortable, my comfort didn't matter. I was also scared of being alone. I was afraid of splitting holidays because I didn't want to be alone. I wanted to stay as close to my in-laws as I could because it was my comfort zone. I already felt like a failure, being divorced at thirty-four years old. I started feeling like I was not meant to be happy. What I wasn't getting was that my happiness was predicated on people, but I needed to be who I was called to be in God. It would take me years to really understand this concept. I was needy and was looking for validation of others subconsciously. So, yes, I had my divorce papers, and I should have felt free, but I still felt the bondage of the broken marriage.

I started to date, figuring I would get over this feeling of failure. But that just got me in more trouble because I wasn't dealing with the deep-rooted issues I was struggling with. And that led me into my first fornication relationship. Yes, now this church girl was fornicating. I justified it by not doing it a lot, only when the sexual feeling was so overwhelming I couldn't take it anymore; then I would get my quick fix. Living two lives was hard because deep down inside, I knew better and knew God's requirements for my life. But I wanted to be wanted. I didn't allow God to make me over and heal me. I would receive a little portion of his spirit and get a glimpse of what he wanted to do in my life, and I would run because I now had that failure attached to my life. These were my thoughts anyway.

In the midst of going through these struggles, I would get myself together so that I would be able to teach Sunday school, lead devotional, aid my aunt, and sing in the choir. God would bless me, but I was so uncomfortable because one thing about me is that I don't like phoniness.

I eventually let that relationship go and immediately got involved with a man I would quickly get engaged to. We didn't even know each other for seven months before we were engaged. I believe because I wouldn't have sex with him, he thought if he asked me to marry him, we would be able to have sex, but he was sadly mistaken. I wasn't attracted to him, but we had fun together and with our children. When you suffer from not feeling worthy, you begin to settle for anything because you feel that's all you are worth. Everyone thought I was crazy because he wasn't a handsome man; he didn't talk much and they could see these hidden sin tendencies. This relationship would secretly cause me to really have a nervous breakdown.

Because I chose not to deal with my issues of neediness, failure, red flags, and low self-esteem, I almost took myself as well as my children over a cliff. There were so many secrets. I tried to cover up certain things because I didn't want to be a failure, and I found someone who wanted me and my children; we were safe around him. I was about to yet again attach myself to another man who had access to generational curses attached to his life. See, when you don't acknowledge and deal with issues and get delivered, you will continue to attract that same spirit to you. Two weeks before we were to walk down the aisle, we had to pick up our wedding license and couldn't because he was already married to two other people. He had been marrying women for money so they could stay in the country. I went into such a deep depression and was so embarrassed that I had gotten not only myself but also the people I love involved in this mess.

This man ended up stealing my engagement ring and money from me. I believe now that the devil was trying to kill me in the spirit. When God has called you, there's nothing the devil won't do to break you. After that experience, I realized that I had to start thinking with my head and not my heart. I had to open eyes so that I would be aware that the thief comes to steal, kill and destroy John 10:10 (NIV) "The thief comes only to steal, kill and destroy; I have come that they may have life, and have it to the full". **How do you deal with embarrassment? How do you deal with regret?**

Real Talk and Reflection

Real Talk and Reflection

Real Talk and Reflection

Chapter 11

2016

From 2015 to 2016, two things happened to me. My uncle and aunt moved to Virginia permanently, and I met a new man who would cause me to grow up and walk into reality.

My aunt's leaving made my issues of abandonment resurface. It was traumatic for me; it was like losing my mother all over again. The bond my aunt and I shared was strong, and not having her around was hard; I was struggling really badly. Secretly I was mad at God but didn't want to admit it. I was being passive-aggressive, and it almost cost me my life.

Meeting him highlighted the hidden sinful tendencies I wasn't addressing in my life. I remember asking God on New Year's Eve 2015 for a change. Never in my wildest dreams did I expect what was going to take place in my life.

I wasn't sure who I was and was asked the question, "Who are you, and what do you like to do?" To my surprise I couldn't answer the question. Other than being a mother, college graduate, and a saved woman, I couldn't really answer the question, and that bothered me. I was forty years old, and I didn't understand who I was and who had God created me to be. I quickly found myself in a new relationship and was looking at life differently.

When I met this man, I already had a mindset of "I'm just going to allow this relationship to flow." I wasn't going to get uptight about sex; I just was going to go with the flow. I will admit that this relationship felt like one of the best relationships I had ever been (a false positive). It was a good relationship, but my relationship with God suffered tremendously. Because I was now fornicating, I felt uncomfortable going to church, reading the word, and praying. I didn't want to be a phony.

This brother had a great job, had his own apartment and car, and dressed well. We had great conversation, and he was family oriented. He taught me so much about life and the game. He had so much insight and wisdom, but he lacked Christian principles and didn't quite understand God fully Amos 3:3 (KJV) "Can two walk together, except they be agreed" which were red flags, but I thought I could convince him to develop a relationship with God. I was in denial. He was an alpha male with a very persuasive personality. I quickly entered into a life of sex and doing wifely duties with no commitment attached. He made me feel like a woman, especially in the bedroom, and didn't care that I was a full-figured woman. Our conversations were about life, business and they helped me to think differently about everything. The only thing I regret is getting further and further into my flesh, leaving my life in Christ in the backburner. I convinced myself that if I loved him and devoted my life to him, he would eventually ask me to be his wife. At the time he was loving me conditionally, and God remained loving me unconditionally.

Again, I didn't allow a man to earn me. I just gave myself freely, thinking I was making grown-woman decisions and making moves. I didn't trust that God could lead this relationship, and turn things around. I didn't stop and think about the big picture. Instead, I was moving further away from my Father in heaven and all that he had predestined me to do for his kingdom. After two years some unfortunate circumstances happened to him, which brought us into a constant unhappy place. The more I would tried to love him, cook for him, have sex with him, or do special things he liked, the more he started to resent and hate me. I continued to try and convince this man to trust in God, but that wasn't where his mindset was. I was playing in the devil's territory and about to be annihilated.

I had walked away from God but was trying to be prayer warrior and uplift him while sinning against the same God I was praying to. Yes, I was living a two-faced lifestyle. It's so important before entering into any relationship that you work on your mind, body, and spirit to avoid constantly bringing brokenness into your life. I knew it was only a matter of time before I was going to have to choose this day whom I was going to serve. When you have tasted the goodness of God, you understand that you can't serve two masters.

God told me to walk away and stand on his promises and principles. In order for any relationship to work, God was going to have to be in the center. It took me a minute, but finally I blocked his number on social media and blocked family members. I loved this man, but I loved God first. It was time to truly trust that what God had for me was mine. People of purpose, we have to begin to read God's word, pray and meditate, and get understanding. For months we didn't speak, and I began to strengthen my relationship with God. I was still going through my fleshly struggles, but I was purposed in my heart that I was going to do differently. I wanted God's will to be done in my life, not my will. God was showing me myself and the things that needed to be delivered and strengthened. God also showed me that I have a voice, and I needed to voice my standards. It wasn't up to other people to figure out my standards.

After a few months, the man hit me up to see how the children and I were doing. I'm not going to lie; I was happy but extremely cautious because we had developed unhealthy patterns in the last two years of our relationship. We had some strong talks that were vulnerable for him and for me. In the past, when I discussed these issues, conflict would occur. This time was different; we both were speaking and being heard by each other. The most important thing, just like I was spending time with God, he was spending time with God as well. His point of view had changed. He began initiating marriage talk and prayer. When the celibacy subject was brought back up, he was with it. We both admitted it wasn't going to be easy due to already having had sex for four and a half years of our relationship. We both purposed in our hearts to read the word, pray, and seek God for true understanding of the importance of waiting for marriage. Real talk it wasn't easy, but it is possible with God. James 4:7 (NIV) states, "Submit yourselves, then to God. Resist the devil, and he will flee from you." And Matthew 17:21 (KJV) states, "Howbeit, this kind goeth not out but by prayer and fasting." That has to become a lifestyle. I don't know where this relationship is going or if it will even last. I do know that I choose God and I receive what he has for my life. My mind, body, and spirit belong to God. I declare, I will not have sex before marriage. **Does your relationships please God?**

Real Talk and Reflection

Real Talk and Reflection

Chapter 12

CALLED TO BE

Being a woman of God and living in real life and experiencing real stuff becomes difficult at times. You can be in church and give God praise one minute and go home and be in the devil's den the next minute. I lived for a long time entertaining the imaginations of my mind. It states in 2 Corinthians 10:5 (KJV) "Casting down imaginations, and every high thing that exalted itself against the knowledge of God, and bringing into captivity every thought to the obedience of Christ."

Every time God would begin to use me spiritually, I would renege because I didn't feel worthy enough. I didn't realize it then, but I know now I felt inadequate to receive anything (insufficient for purpose), and I kept going through life like the children of Israel, not believing God's plan over my life. I didn't fully understand what curses over my life meant, and not understanding, I didn't know how to get them off my life.

Walking in the wilderness and continuing working in ministry, going to work, mothering my children, and being a woman, I was neglecting and abandoning who God created me to be. I didn't understand the call on my life. I was dealing with so much other stuff that I could not hear, smell, and taste what God had for my life. I was in a space of being trapped in bondage, only being released occasionally. I didn't believe who God said that I was. I would act like I believed, but my actions showed the truth. The power of God scared me and exposed those things that were comforting to me. I felt that as long as I did nice things for people, that was my calling, but it wasn't God's best for me. I was dealing with other people's problems and issues but wouldn't touch mine. I took two young ladies into my home and mothered them and was doing what I thought was God's work. It was nice but not God's best for my life. It wasn't my job. God placed three lives in my hands plus my own, and I was neglecting all of them and not dealing with what God wanted me to. Instead I was being distracted and in someone else's business and neglecting God's plan over my life. Ultimately I should have been minding my own business, allowing God to fix my issues, and not trying to fix others' issues like I was God. Being in bondage, I was tied up; I couldn't fight and resist distractions. I identified with the inadequacies in others' lives and thought it was my job to fix them. I was living in a system called limiting beliefs; which prevented me from living, believing and operating in who God created me to be. I was operating in fear which led to lack of motivation, chronic procrastination, and lack of internal resources. God is a jealous God, and anyone trying to take his place will be dealt with. And God will expose and destroy because it was never ordained in the first place. I learned that minding my business would bring me to my breakthrough.

I had to adopt the "Speak life into it" lifestyle. I began to write the vision and make it plain. Everything that concerned me, I spoke life into. Anything that I knew was a stronghold, I totally gave to God. I didn't know how I was going to stop fornicating. I took it to God and said, "Lord, I will stop sleeping with this man, even if it means the relationship has to end because it's not a healthy relationship." God made way that we were spending less time together, and then we wouldn't talk for weeks. During that time God was building me up and making me stronger until it got to the point where I spoke it out of my mouth that I no longer was going to be living in fornication. I was not afraid to be alone and without a boyfriend. I was finally ready to take my rightful place in the kingdom. God delivered me from the spirit of inadequacy. My eyes were opened; I could now see in the spirit. My ears were opened; I could hear in the spirit. I understood my self-worth and that my life didn't belong to me, but it was created to be used by God.

All of these experiences taught me to appreciate God and that I am his child. They taught me that I've been placed in this world for such a time as now. I learned to deal with conflicts and forgive. I've learned to appreciate what God gave me at birth: my biological family. I had to learn that not dealing with my issues didn't change anything. Today I appreciate and love that God blessed me with a family who loves me. I'm no longer running from my past. One of my biggest things I'm grateful for is building relationships with my father, stepmother, beautiful sisters Shanise, Tonya, and Sauda. I didn't realize how much I needed them in my life.

These experiences taught me that God loves me and I was born to honor him. I wasn't a mistake, my children weren't mistakes and every unfortunate thing I experienced God was going to work it together for his good.

I exposed my life because I am ready to live free and realized that I went through these difficult things to be able to help someone else in the process. I've learned that I had to stop holding secrets and wearing a mask. The more I thought about it I had to ask myself; **why did I hide?**

I am free, a woman, an entrepreneur, a mother, a daughter, a sister, a niece, a cousin, an aunt, and a friend, but I've been called to be a woman of God, an author, a life coach, a motivational speaker, a teacher, a preacher, and a furious warrior. Writing this book has allowed me to walk in my truth, have a voice and be healed.

I pray all that have read this book have been blessed, received insight, and been set free and now will begin to walk in your truth in mind, body, and spirit. Know that no matter what you had to go through in this life, it was for your good. Trust that God got you. Last but not least, it's time for us all to walk in our destiny, not away from it. **Who are you? Are you wearing a mask? Are you hiding secrets?**

Real Talk and Reflection

Real Talk and Reflection

Real Talk and Reflection

About the Author

Living my life healthy mind, body, and spirit. These are vibrant words of author, motivational speaker, life coach, and entrepreneur T. J. Callahan. A single mother of three wonderful children, she has always prided herself on being a fun, down-to-earth and hardworking woman who takes care of her business as a mom and businesswoman.

T. J. Callahan obtained her Bachelor of Arts in public relations and marketing at Ashford University. Currently, she is a harm reduction specialist working in the community with individuals currently dealing with homelessness, AIDS, HIV, mental health issues, and substance use.

While attending Morning Star Full Gospel Assembly in the Bronx, New York, T. J. Callahan discovered her gift in motivating people, especially youth and women, to be more than what society limited them to be. She was instrumental in cofounding a mentoring program for youth ages seven to eighteen called Sister to Sister and Bond with Your Brother. She facilitated conflict resolution and esteem enhancement workshops as well as recreational activities. This motivated T. J. Callahan to begin several rites-of-passage classes for young ladies called Daughters of Destiny and to become a prominent leader in women's ministry.

In addition to being a motivational speaker, T. J. Callahan is co-owner and managing senior partner of Eighteen50 Apparel, an empowerment apparel company consisting of two partners who provide knowledge and power by teaching black history through fashion. Her main responsibilities are overseeing the marketing, operational, and creative direction and budgets for all the products that are sold.

Recently, T. J. Callahan has become an author of the book *The Real Life of a Church Girl: The Untold Story*. It is a biography about her life growing up as a church girl and all the lessons she learned and the trials she overcame.

www.ingramcontent.com/pod-product-compliance
Ingram Content Group UK Ltd.
Pitfield, Milton Keynes, MK11 3LW, UK
UKHW022240230426
12048UKWH00018BA/1384